If you purchased this book without a cover, you should be aware that this book is stolen property. It was reported as "unsold and destroyed" to the publisher, and the author has not received payment for this "stripped book."

ISBN Number: 0-61537-322-4

Take It from Her: Cautionary Lessons for the Ladies We Love

Copyright © 2010 Tremayne Moore
www.maynetre.com
Published by Maynetre Manuscripts, LLC

All rights reserved. Except for use in the case of brief quotations embodied in critical articles and reviews, the reproduction or utilization of this work in whole or part in any form by any electronic, digital, mechanical or other means, now known or hereafter invented, including xerography, photocopying, scanning, recording, or any information storage or retrieval system, is forbidden without written prior permission of the author and publisher, Maynetre Manuscripts, LLC.

The scanning, uploading, and distribution of this book via the Internet or via any other means without permission of the publisher and author is illegal and punishable by law. Purchase only authorized versions of this book, and do not participate in or encourage electronic piracy of copyrighted materials. Your support of the author's rights is appreciated.

This is a work of fiction. Names, characters, places, and incidents are products of the author's imagination, the author's own personal experience, or are used fictitiously and are not to be construed as real. While the author was inspired in part by actual events, the characters are not distantly inspired by any individual known or unknown to the author. Any resemblance to actual events, locales, business establishments, organizations, or persons, living or dead, is entirely coincidental.

The author makes no apology for how the very **REAL** presence of God in this work of fiction may impact the reader's spiritual life.

Printed in the United States of America
First Printing 2010
10 9 8 7 6 5 4 3 2 1

Edited by Shantae A. Charles www.shantaecharles.com
Cover Design: ROC Studios International, Inc.

What Readers Are Saying About Take It from Her

This book speaks to the heart of women. From trials and pain, to God's healing power and restoration, the author's poems express what for many women is a sad reality as they look for love in all the wrong places. It also reveals the gifts of mercy and grace, given to us freely by our Heavenly Father. 'Take it from Her' is a wake-up call and a call to action for of us to find our worth, strength and hope in God's promises rather than on the fleeting desires of the flesh.

- *Cynthia M. Portalatin*

This book is a collection of poems depicting the varied experiences of women and brings them together by lyrically and profoundly encapsulating our encounters. The level of familiarity is so great that you will reflect, relate, and be renewed as it reveals hard facts and spiritual truths. A journey through the pages of this book, finds each chapter taking you down the hallway of self discovery. It draws you into a proverbial place where doors will open and you are revealed. Peer poetically into the rooms of life and find your place in its pages. Enter, Examine, Evolve, Enjoy, and You will be Blessed!

- *Andréa S. Bailey*

Take It From Her: Cautionary Lessons for the Ladies We Love

Tremayne Moore

Published by Maynetre Manuscripts, LLC

Acknowledgments

First and foremost, I give all thanks and praise to my Lord and Savior Jesus Christ. Thank You for salvation and the gift of Your Son. You are doing exceeding abundantly above all that I could ever ask or think. And for that I'm grateful and overwhelmed, knowing well enough that I don't deserve your goodness.

To my immediate and extended family – I love all of you.

A heartfelt thanks goes to the following people: Brigitte Marshall for your contribution to this book; Robert & Shantae Charles for keeping me on deadlines, editing this book, writing a wonderful foreword, the great cover and photos, and anything else I failed to mention (you've done it again, and it's all God); my beautiful "Cover Girls" (you know who you are - smile) who appeared on the cover; Cynthia Portalatin for your contributions to this book and proofreading this; and to all of the ladies (especially Andréa S. Bailey) who provided constructive feedback, who threw topics at me to write about and most importantly for being who you are, wonderful in God's image (smile).

I want to extend my sincerest gratitude to the following individuals (who have sown into my life): Sisters Marilynn Griffith, Sharon Ewell Foster, Barbara Williams & Stanice Anderson – thank you for challenging me as a writer, speaking words of encouragement, and sharing your wisdom to up and coming authors at the SistaFaith Conference; my sister and fellow author Dawn Bruce – I am blessed to meet you and God has so much in store for you; my sister and fellow author Melodie Kent, congrats on your book <u>Finding Her</u> – I loved it! You are one talented sister, and I am so blessed that you're my friend. My brother and fellow author Michael Beckford – brother, it's no accident that God allowed us to cross paths. Your drive is an encouragement to me, and although I may not say it, I do appreciate you sharing your knowledge about this business. Sister Katina Amoah – we've known each other for roughly twelve years, and we've seen a lot of things. As a result, WE CAN (get it) make a difference.

I would like to extend my appreciation and love to all of the ministries and church families that have supported my ministry.

To the young ladies at Pace Leon – thanks for keeping it real and having a listening ear during your poetry recital.

If I didn't mention your name, charge it to my head and not my heart.

Special Thanks

To my entire Four Oaks Community Church family (Pastor Erik & Tori Braun) – Tallahassee, Florida, (www.fouroakschurch.com), you are the essence of Agape love. You have opened your homes and hearts to me, and I thank God for all of you. God has so much more in store for us individually and as a Church. To my pastors at Four Oaks, thank you for preaching the unadulterated word of God and feeding the flock. It is a privilege and honor to call you my pastors.

Foreword

There are many issues that women face: abuse, discrimination, misrepresentation are just a few. This book of prose seeks to shed light on some of those issues while imparting hope and inspiration. Tremayne does an incredible job delving into the psyche of women and honorably displaying not only the plight of women around the globe but also the triumphs of women at their best. As I read, I took inventory of myself, my peers, and my own treatment of the women around me. This book is not just well written prose, but an eye and ear opener for everyone who can read the lines and the meaning that lies between them.

Shantae A. Charles
Editor-In-Chief

Author's Foreword

When I was given the title for this book by my editor, I didn't have to think too hard to write poems from a woman's viewpoint. With so many shows on television and my association with so many women, I would hear so many stories. These stories would range from lovely to horrific. In fact, I was recently asked by a young lady (in her teens), what do I know about women? Well, I was privileged to share some poems from this book, and God spoke to the young ladies whom I was sharing with. The more I think about it, another woman asked me after reading a poem from this book, "Are you going to put on a wig and assume a pseudonym? It's kind of scary how right you are with these poems." My response to that is simply, it's all God and not me.

With that said, I pray that you open your heart to His Spirit and that you will allow Him to minister to you. Finally, I pray that you are blessed, highly favored & empowered to prosper under His hand.

For His glory,

Tremayne Moore

Dedication:

My grandmother Joyce Springer

To every woman!

Table of Contents

Room 1: The Closet...10
1. Butterfly (Monica's Theme)..11
2. I'm Not Good Enough...12
3. Little Miss Heartbreaker..14
4. Men...15
5. The Tyrant (Ladies Version)...16

Room 2: The Powder Room...17
1. I Am Beautiful...18
2. Learn From Me..19
3. My Friend..20
4. My Love For You..21

Room 3: The Dressing Room...23
1. A Woman's Body...24
2. My Worth As A Woman..25
3. Running Away...26
4. The Embarrassment..27
5. Why The Drama?...28
6. Your Freedom...29

Room 4: The Board Room..30
1. A Better Place...31
2. I Need Balance...33
3. It's All About Me..34
4. Mother's Day...35
5. Still Here...36
6. The Big Payback..38
7. This Is Me (A Woman's Declaration)...39
8. What Did I Gain?...40

Room 5: The Bedroom...41
1. A Sister's Commitment To Purity (Piece And Purity).........................42

    2. Blame It On Love..43

    3. I Need A Man (Parts 1 & 2)..................................44

    4. Someone To Love..47

    5. The Life Of Alyssa Cooper (Parts 1 & 2).............49

Room 6: The Bridal Suite...51

    1. Don't Waste My Time..52

    2. He's The One/She's The One..............................53

    3. Saying Good-bye (The Separation) (Parts 1 & 2).....55

    4. She's Gone (Parts 1 & 2).....................................57

    5. Skin Deep..58

    6. This Feeling..59

    7. When It's Your Turn (This Feeling pt. 2)............60

    8. Wedding Dreams...61

    9. Who Do You Love?..62

Room 7: The Secret Place...63

    1. Accept Me Broken (Let Love Make Me Whole).......64

    2. Grief..65

    3. I Can't Take This Anymore..................................66

    4. I Feel So..67

    5. Listen To Me...68

    6. The Conversion...69

    7. The Sanctity Of Life..70

Room 8: The Delivery Room...71

    1. Dream Again...72

    2. New Identity...73

    3. Pregnant Is My Name..74

About The Author..75

Room 1: The Closet

Take It From Her: Cautionary Lessons for the Ladies We Love

Butterfly (Monica's Theme)

Once upon a time, a caterpillar enters the world.
Yes, this caterpillar is symbolic for a beautiful girl.
She was protected in a jar, with a family who crushed her dearly.
As she progressed towards the butterfly stage, her beauty was displayed clearly.

Before reaching that stage in totality, she endured heartaches and tears.
She was a victim of foul play; it seemed no one could calm her fears.
When she fully blossomed, her family set her free.
She is now free to fly, free to be herself, free to see who she is meant to be.

Another tragedy occurs, and she's trapped in a different jar.
The tears occur again, for she wanted to go far.
In this jar, she would face cruelty and undeserved abuse.
What's left to do, other than to give in thinking, "what's the use?"

Eventually, she's set free again, this time with a renewed power.
She's learning to fly further, every minute and every hour.
I happen to see her as she flies gracefully in the sky,
And I think, she's beautiful, and she can surely fly.

When I catch her, I see the tears she's cried,
And I ensure my jar is safe and secure; I sure tried
To comfort, love and protect her from those who don't care.
But would she give me a chance? She wouldn't dare.

After a few days, she's so determined to be free.
But what can I do? I must let her be.
I will say that I love you and watch as you kiss the sky.
Spread your wings my sister, for you are a treasured butterfly.

Take It From Her: Cautionary Lessons for the Ladies We Love

I'm Not Good Enough

Cassandra is my co-worker; she's narrow-minded and she knows everything.
Cheri is the new employee; she's attractive and she can truly sing.
Working with Cassandra can be confrontational and sometimes frustrating.
Maybe she gets a thrill out of this; to me it's irritating.
I would introduce myself to Cheri and would find out she's from my hometown.
We bonded as co-workers, nothing serious, but Cassandra won't let me live it down.
Cassandra thinks I'm interested in Cheri; so she blatantly says to me, "I'm not good enough."
She says I'm this; I'm that; I'm not a true Christian or a real man, and all that stuff.

I could talk to Cheri for twenty minutes, and Cassandra would blatantly interrupt our conversation
To talk to her for four hours! Now that *really* raises my frustration.
I overheard the discussion, and Cassandra says to Cheri, "I know someone who's perfect for you--
He goes to my church, and I think you'll like him too,"
After she leaves Cheri's office, she drops by my office to say "She's off limits!
I'm going to protect her from people like you, and your time with her is finished!"
Cassandra arranges a date for Cheri and this man to meet at eight.
She told Cheri to give her details when it's over; Cheri said "OK," and Cassandra said "Great!"

Little did Cassandra know, this man is a rapist on warrant in two states.
I found this out from my friends, but I felt my chance to stop this was too late.
It would be indeed, and Cheri was off to this stranger's home.
I said, "I'm way better than him, and I hope Cassandra's happy now that they're alone."
The man says, "If you don't lay down with me, I'll put a cap in your head."
So, to avoid being killed, Cheri lies down with her back to the bed.

Take It From Her: Cautionary Lessons for the Ladies We Love

He then puts the gun aside and proceeds to rape her in the most horrific way.
She thought, "Why did I let Cassandra play matchmaker, when I could've taken time to pray?"

She's screaming please stop for ten minutes, and again he places his gun to her head.
This time he fires a bullet. Pow! Cheri is pronounced dead!

Some may think this telling too graphic.
Some may think this telling so lame.
But no one is thinking the hardest question of all:
Who is really to blame?

Small group idea:
Put together 3 groups.
Defend your point of view on who is to blame.

Take It From Her: Cautionary Lessons for the Ladies We Love

Little Miss Heartbreaker

Hey ladies, we are some fine women, aren't we?
And these men need to appreciate the beauty of you and me.
We are heartbreakers, and we can get what we want.
Money, jewelry, love, and affection, and their minds we surely can taunt.

Let me tell you my story, as Little Miss Heartbreaker.
You all know we're 100% woman, and none of us here are fakers.
I would go from one man to another, playing two men at the same time.
I would make them bow down to me and say, what's yours is mine.

They wouldn't argue or raise a fuss, because I had their hearts in my hand.
I'm so good at this; at the beach, I had about five men as my fan.
I'd tell them I loved them, and they would flock to my commands.
Just steady teasing them, and of course, I took their hearts and ran.

I felt that if I didn't get my way, I would throw a tantrum like a child.
Of course, it was total manipulation, but it was surely worthwhile.
Men can do it to women; so, why shouldn't I do it to them?
I have a plus, my beauty is fatal; I'm priceless as a gem.

My problem came when one man didn't appreciate me breaking his heart.
He was so obsessed with me that he would eventually rip me apart.
He beat me up, literally, with marks on my face and abdomen.
I pressed charges and had to reconsider how my behavior had been.

Being Little Miss Heartbreaker isn't worth it; you can be cute but think about others.
No man should be any woman's slave; if you think he is, run for cover.
I thought that, and now can you see my bruises from that situation.
Learn from me, and straighten your life; I hope this will spread throughout this nation.

Take It From Her: Cautionary Lessons for the Ladies We Love

Men

I had a past that you would never understand.
I was molested at eight, and would vow to never date a man.
I planned to be single for life, but that plan would change.
At the age of twelve, my life would be rearranged.

I was molested again by a relative, and my family took their side.
So, I tried to find a safe place where I could run and hide.

School life was interesting; I'd get the same old line from boys.
Saying, "Ooh baby, you're so fine, you bring me so much joy"

And like a typical girl, I fell for that line.
Only to fall into this trap time after time.

Now, here I stand with three children, all from different men.
I hate men, and I blame God for all of my sin.

Where was He? He could've protected me like a real father.
People say to me, "Give your burdens to Him," and I say, "Why bother?"

I'm in a relationship now, and this man beats me like I'm his African Drum.
I must be helplessly trapped because he's such a great lover...to some.

I leave him after he abuses me, but I still take him back.
He says, "You'll never find another like me," and I toughen up for his attacks.
People now say, "Why do you allow this again and again?"
Because I'm looking for love, but deep inside, I still hate men!

Take It From Her: Cautionary Lessons for the Ladies We Love

The Tyrant (Ladies Version)

When I met this man, he was fine and all that I needed to complete me.
I did everything I could to ensure that he would keep me.
I turned my back on my friends; I didn't hear their concerns or cries.
I really didn't trust the Lord either; I just didn't want this new love to die.

Well, we married in a short period of time, and he took off his mask.
He became very demanding, and had me do multiple tasks.
I had to cater to him, and everything had to receive his approval.
Yeah, my true friends were worried; they overlooked my distance and removal.

I took offense to what my friends were trying to speak into my life.
All that mattered? I was the Tyrant's Wife.
He would call me names and belittle me in front of my kids.
Just to prove his manhood; I was allowing him to do what he did.

He would choose my friends; ask me everywhere I've been.
When we were out in public, I was not allowed to look at other men.
I had to look at the ground, and he would use words to abuse me.
I would feel like a slave at times, and I allowed him to serve me a full course of misery.

The light bulb finally went off, and God now has my attention.
Why are you enduring this, and I also need to mention
The friends you pushed off were praying for you to be free
Now I'm divorced, no longer the Tyrant's Wife; and it feels good to be freely me.

Take It From Her: Cautionary Lessons for the Ladies We Love

Room 2: The Powder Room

Take It From Her: Cautionary Lessons for the Ladies We Love

I Am Beautiful

Look at me, I'm 100% woman, and beautiful in the eyes of the Most High.
He has blessed me by giving me His breath of life, and I feel like I can fly.
I am beautiful, loved, and no one has to talk me out of it.
No one can tell me otherwise, I have so much to live for, and I just won't quit.

I look at women today, and it's disheartening what my eyes see.
Some women have to spend money on clothes to express their originality.
They failed to see no clothes define a woman's beauty and love.
A woman's beauty comes from knowing that you have been blessed by God above.

Some women feel their beauty comes from makeup on their face,
But they failed to realize their heart is never hidden when then go from place to place.
Do you need to wear it at all times and everywhere you go?
Every part of your body is beautiful "as is;" that's something you need to know.

Some women do all kinds of things to themselves to attract a mate.
Is this for your glory or God's? Are you flirting just to get a date?
Does having a man determine that you're beautiful? When will we ladies learn?
Your beauty comes from who you serve; that should make His head turn.

I am beautiful, because God loves me, and that's all I need to know.
I'm free to live for Him, and I want His love in me to grow.
I encourage you sisters to stop the unnecessary drama in your world.
Rather than being catty, share your beauty with your girls!

It's time out for looking outward when really in the end.
Beauty is not skin deep; beauty is within!

Take It From Her: Cautionary Lessons for the Ladies We Love

Learn From Me

Please don't land in my situation; your spirit needs to be free.
Learn from me; so your life won't go through the misery.
So many of us want a man who's got some roughness in him,
But learn from me so your spiritual light doesn't become dim.

I had a man; he said things I wanted to hear.
I gave in and thought my gray skies would miraculously become clear.
At first, it started great, but we got into a physical altercation.
He beat me like I was his enemy, and said this was my initiation.

He said, "In this relationship, you submit to me, and will do everything I say.
I wear the pants; you can't look or talk to other men, and if you do, you'll pay.
I can have relations with other women; yes, they can be my ex-girlfriends.
You will watch me and have nothing to say, and if you do, your life will end!"

If he had a bad day at work, I would be his punching bag.
He would beat me for not cooking to his satisfaction, or if I looked like a hag.
I was not to work, but still be his trophy; I felt like a domestic slave.
I was to give him anything he wanted, to satisfy his every last crave.

We got into another altercation, and I kicked him in his groin.
I flew out the house, running and screaming, not sure of where I was going.
A woman rescued me and hid me from this jealous dictator.
I finally came to my senses and said, "How can this man be such a woman hater?"
No woman needs a dictator in her life, she needs a God-fearing man.
A man who will treasure her, love her and take her by the hand.

Take It From Her: Cautionary Lessons for the Ladies We Love

My Friend

(This was written in 8 minutes. I learned this technique at a writer's conference – if you can carve out 8 minutes a day, you'll be astonished at how much you can write.)

Here we go again; what I have done has made you mad.
And every time this occurs, I'm the one who ends up sad.
It's either something I've foolishly said or done; I uttered the first thought on my mind.
But you let me have it, because I burned you, and loneliness is what I find.

I know the goofy trait is embedded in my personality,
But I do know how to separate fantasy from reality.
Do I need to be direct with you, or could I be humorous around you?
I know you know my heart, and that you'll allow my love to surround you.

I know that I'm not perfect; please don't hold that against me.
Your friendship means the world to me, and hopefully this you'll undoubtedly see.
This is brief and straightforward, but my love for you will never end.
I cherish, admire and esteem you, and I'm honored to call you my friend.

Take It From Her: Cautionary Lessons for the Ladies We Love

My Love For You

I see you as you wake each morn.
You dread getting out of bed; wrapping yourself with forlorn.
You're thinking, "Why do I have to get in my car to go to work?
I have to endure some trifling people; they're nothing but jerks!"

As you carry on through your day, I long to commune with you.
I just don't want your bad days; I also want your good days, too.
I see you and cry, because I love you and want to show you
That this love I have for you is real, even though I already know you.

I know sometimes you can grieve my heart.
Don't think that I'll reject you; my love for you will not depart.
No matter how you treat me, my love for you is real.
Don't be afraid of me, and don't be reluctant to tell me how you feel.

I want to be more than a friend to you and wrap my arms around you.
You can try to hide from me or avoid me; please let my love surround you.
You can cover your face with makeup, but you can't hide your heart.
And I know deep inside that your heart is torn apart.

It's Me who brought you this far.
It's Me who defines who you are.
Don't ever say to yourself that you're self-made.
For I sent my Son for you, and it was your debt He paid.

Don't dare to think you can make it on your own.
For without Me you will struggle, and without Me you are alone.
I would hate to see you go through another day without Me.
You can only go so far; if only this truth you would see.

I would love to be able to spend time with you.
I just don't want your bad days; I want your good days too.
Allow this love I have to embrace your face like the morning air.
Let it whisper to your soul: that as the apple of my eye, I care.

Take It From Her: Cautionary Lessons for the Ladies We Love

You're too special to throw your life away.
You're too special to want to end your life today.
I want you to set your mind on the things which are above.
What more do I have to say and do to prove to you my love?

The greatest love of all is not for you to love yourself.
The greatest love of all is to share it with someone else.
Don't let people tell you that you need to love yourself,
We're to love and be loved by Christ and no one else.

My love for you is genuine; let me pamper and adorn you.
Open your heart to me; let this torrent of love consume.
If you want to go on without me, and if you think love in this world you'll find.
Know that I'll always be here for you, but I plead that you don't get left behind.

Take It From Her: Cautionary Lessons for the Ladies We Love

Room 3: The Dressing Room

Take It From Her: Cautionary Lessons for the Ladies We Love

A Woman's Body
(Dedicated to teenage women)

Hey girls, let's have a heart to heart chat about keeping our bodies in check.
We are blessed to have them, and we need to show them some respect.
The world is trying to demonize them, and we need to change this view.
When you look in the mirror, God made you; signed, sealed and approved.

Some of you may feel you're in a woman's body, but you're still a child.
When you know for certain that God loves you, that should make you smile.
He demands respect for how you conduct yourself, so walk in that pride.
Your body is the temple of His Spirit; and His Spirit should cause you to confidently stride.

Some of you may know boys who want to touch you and give you affection.
They're trying to gain a foothold and make your head spin in all directions.
It's not a sign of endearment; they have a quota to fill.
They want you to surrender your thoughts and desires to their will.

And once they acquire that, all of your respect is out the window.
Some of you will feel crushed and wished no one else would know.
A woman's body belongs to God, and don't forget that girls.
You have a God-given destiny that needs to be fulfilled for your sake and the world's.

Take It From Her: Cautionary Lessons for the Ladies We Love

My Worth as a Woman

Look at her; she's got so much worth and potential in this world.
Why shouldn't she be a mature woman instead of acting like a little girl?
She's chasing men who are going nowhere in life.
They're looking for a playmate and not a wife.

She came to me complaining wondering why she can't find love,
And each one she's been with, she swore it was from above.
"I thought he loved me, and I allowed him to mistreat me.
I'm still alone and allowing these trifling and immature men to cheat me."

I asked her, "Have you ever met a good man?
A man who loves God and loves you the best that he can?"
She said, "Yeah, but I see them as wimps, and they're too nice to me.
They're too easy to take advantage of; I need someone who's rough, you see."

"They don't have to be rough; just for a man to have that image turns me on!"
I said, "Then why do you complain when they use you, discard you, then they're gone?"
She evaded the question, and then I said, "What do you think of my man?"
She said, "He's your type, not mine! He would carry you in the sand."

I said, "Do you have enough worth to believe that you can have this too?"
She said, "Don't pull that religious talk on me; I know you,"
I said, "Well...," she doesn't answer and storms out my door.
When will we ladies understand that God has so much for us in store?

My worth as a woman is defined by Christ and not by anything or anyone on this earth.
Yes, I have a man; he compliments me and vice versa, but God has determined my worth!

Take It From Her: Cautionary Lessons for the Ladies We Love

Running Away

I was talking to a woman the other day.
And out of the blue, she started crying and had this to say:

"What am I doing? I have a child and the baby's dad is a jerk.
He doesn't pay child support and refuses to work.
I had a different boyfriend not too long after, but the relationship died.
He committed innumerable wrongs, from stealing to telling lies.

A few months later, I decided to walk the aisle and wed,
Just to experience the covenant of the wedding bed.
That was the only time this new man was interested in me.
Even though I have the same need, I thought he would be
Everything I needed in a man, except I couldn't change him.
I tried hard to convert and rearrange him,
But the marriage was pure hell, and we separated.
Divorce ensued, and that was complicated.

It's sad that after three months, the marriage went to hell.
I'm trying to tell myself I can break free from this spell.
Although, I don't believe I'm running away from my issues.
Would you excuse me for a minute? I need to grab some tissue.
So a month after my divorce, I found another man.
I told myself I'm going to do the best I can
To keep him regardless of how he treats me.
I really didn't care if he cheats or even beats me.

I just need a man to make me feel loved,
Who will accept me for me, and make me feel it's from above.
Well, he fooled around, and here I am alone.
So, what am I doing wrong? I'm tired of being on my own!"

I believe she's running away from her problems and fears,
And now, I'm emotionally involved, comforting her and drying her tears.

Take It From Her: Cautionary Lessons for the Ladies We Love

The Embarrassment

Here I stand, ashamed, embarrassed, and alone.
I wish someone would ring my phone.
I thought I had it all, the man of my dreams,
Only to find that it was all imagery; so it seems.

I wanted to be married, and vowed it would be forever.
I promised to God that my man and I would be together.
It was fine at first, but I noticed a change in the relationship.
This wasn't right, and one of us needed to dip.

I wanted it to be forever; I wanted it to stand through thick and thin,
But much to my dismay, this relationship came to an end.
How can I stand before God knowing we broke the vow?
I want to hide from people, because I see the truth now.

I didn't wait on God; my flesh needed companionship and love.
I wanted to show people my trophy. What was I thinking of?
I know God will still use me through this experience, even though I'm on my own.
Meanwhile, I still stand here; ashamed, embarrassed, and alone.

Take It From Her: Cautionary Lessons for the Ladies We Love

Why the Drama?

Why can't we all just get along?
Is that asking too much, or do I need to sing an old church song?
Why is there so much drama around me?
Can't I live my life? What do I have to do to show you and the world I'm free?

Sure, you're my biological mother, and you gave birth to a baby girl,
But you will never know the pain I felt as I endured heartaches from this world.
You placed other relatives over me, yet you portrayed us as the perfect family.
How dare you tell such a lie to your friends, and then condone lies from me?

I'm just grateful that I had people, who I consider my parents, listening to me.
They loved me and took me in; this is something you'll never see.
Why did you wish I was never born? Why did you run around in the streets?
What did I ever do to you? You know that I love you and would wash your feet.

Now that I'm older, and I've made it in this world, you want me to bail you out.
And like a little child, when I don't supply your *greed*, you want to scream and shout.
I understand that you are downright selfish, but why the drama, Mom? Why?
Pleasing you is an exercise in futility, and I wonder sometimes why I even try.

When things are good in my life, you want to be in my world,
But when things are bad in my life, you point the finger and disown yo' baby girl.
Why are you so full of drama, giving our gender an infamous name?
You've played the drama card too many times; game over – it's time to change!

Take It From Her: Cautionary Lessons for the Ladies We Love

Your Freedom

Something went wrong; I'm not sure what I said
But knowing me, I blurted out something without using my head
Our friendship was beautiful, and I thought you were everything to me
But as usual, I'm wrong, and you said you want to be free.

You see the look on my face, and you can tell my spirit's troubled.
I feel like I lost my reason for living, and you burst my bubble.
I don't know what my life will be like with you; I'm not sure what I'll do.
I know your search for freedom is important; it's important to me too.

I don't know if you know or even care about the misery I'm going to face,
But that's irrelevant, maybe I should get a one-way ticket to space.
Would that make you happy? I don't know, but nothing is what I am without you.
Everything is beautiful with you, and my whole world is about you.

I dread hearing the words good-bye, but maybe it had to come today.
I don't want you to see me cry, and I'll withhold the words I want to say.
So if you ever find this poem and you desire to read this,
Just know your love towards me is truly missed.

If you ever need a friend, I'll be there for you.
I hope you found your freedom, and every dream that you wish for comes true.
Maybe you feel that right now we're not meant to be.
So I'll try to go on without you, but know that because I love you, I respect your need to find that place called free.

Room 4: The Board Room

Take It From Her: Cautionary Lessons for the Ladies We Love

A Better Place

I see your hurts, and I know how you feel.
It's hard for you to imagine that what you see today is for real.
I understand we're living in what we call today, Survival 101,
And the people who are scoffing and mocking are having tons of fun.

It seems it's better to go with the majority even though they're not doing right.
I know for me, I'm ready to take up my armor and fight.
What would I gain? Nothing, so I change how I think about this matter,
Even though I'm aware my enemies want my head on a silver platter.

Will selfishness, envy, strife and its cousins stop? For me, it's hard to tell.
Every time I wake up, it seems as if I'm walking into a living hell.
Job stress, people stress, the world is falling; I know this feeling well.
I try to look for that silver lining, in the midst of my dry spell.

I'd rather suffer for doing right than to suffer for doing wrong.
I know what I'm facing today won't be this way for long.
My weeping may endure for a night; joy will come in the morning light.
For if I'm doing what's right and walking in God's favor, I'll win this fight.

I can't control what others do, but I choose to keep my eyes on a better place
Where I will be free to be me and no tears will be on my face.
But until then, I will know that this world is fallen and the end is near.
If we don't look at ourselves and change, how can we stand to live another year?

This world can take my job, my friends, my career, and other material things,
But they can't take the hope of a better place and flying on eagle's wings.

Take It From Her: Cautionary Lessons for the Ladies We Love

I know my enemies will stand before God, receiving their payback.
Meanwhile, I will relax and let my enemies continue with their futile attacks.

As I hope in a better place, I'll let God's favor carry me through,
And pray that you will allow God's favor and love to carry you too.
I know God has the final say so as to what happens in my life,
And until He calls me home, I'll endure the pain and strife.

I know He is in control, and He has a better place prepared for me.
I will not let my heart be troubled as I long for the day where I'll be free.
In closing: I will live life so my name in His book of life won't be erased,
And I would love to see you there when He calls us to our better place.

Take It From Her: Cautionary Lessons for the Ladies We Love

I Need Balance

My life is in such chaos, turmoil and in total disarray.
What did I do to cause this? What did I let stand in the way?
Is it my ministry, my friends or not spending time with the Most High?
I need balance in my life; for without it, I will surely die.

I see so many marriages crumble, because their ministry dominates their life.
I know I have a ministry, but I also have responsibilities as a mother and wife.
My husband loves me, and I love him, and that's something I'll shout about
It seems like I'm carrying a load, and at the end of the day, I'm burnt out.

Lord I need balance; I don't want to lose my first love for you.
I guess the first thing I need to do is turn to Your Word and pray like I used to.
I was a woman on fire for God, but I let the cares of the world take me over.
I know when I turn to You for help; you bring me back to reality like a long lost lover.

Lord I need balance; I don't want my family to precede my ministry.
My husband is my backbone, and we have a wonderful chemistry.
I feel so embarrassed that I'm at this breaking point in my life,
But I submit to you Lord, and also to my husband to be his helping wife.

If I need to put some things on hold, I'll humbly swallow my pride.
I know You have a purpose for all this, although I feel as if I'm dying inside.
You gave me this family for a reason, and the devil will not break us up.
You made family, then church; so help me drink this cup.

Without You first in my life, I'm out of balance and out of touch.
Although I may be blessed externally, internally I don't have much.
I understand that my family is also a ministry that's of importance to You.
So, my prayer to You Lord is that you bring balance and order in all I do.

Take It From Her: Cautionary Lessons for the Ladies We Love

It's All About Me

It's all about me, and that is so right.
To know that men do what I say is out of sight.
I control the tempo; I control the relationship.
If any man doesn't like it; he can dip!

I don't have to apologize for anything I do.
You are beneath me, and I don't have to kiss up to you.
Men have to bow down at my feet and kiss the ground I walk on.
It's all about me, and my beauty is something to look upon.

Yeah, I'm fine and can get anything my heart and flesh desires.
I can take any man's heart and mind through the fire.
While I'm on it, I also don't have to accept any man's apology if I don't want to.
The decision is mine, and there's nothing you can do.

I see so many women stepped on, and I'm going to take a stand.
It's going to be all about me from now on, and that's what I expect from a man.
He will cater to my every whim, and he's going to enjoy every moment of it.
If not, I will throw a tantrum and give a Broadway performance.

Men are idiotic and clueless, and I love the nice men whom I can use.
They are so sensitive and caring; (laughing devilishly) those are the easy ones to abuse.
I call the shots, and I love dogging men when I'm talking with my girls on the phone.
But every night I still face one question: why, oh why am I still alone?

Take It From Her: Cautionary Lessons for the Ladies We Love

Mother's Day

This is for all mothers of the world, for you ought to be celebrated.
Your position as a mother is truly underrated.
You are the helper, provider, nurturer, and other things unmentioned.
And when you speak with a quiet spirit, you deserve all the attention.

When the family needs help, you're the one the family turns to.
Your love for the family is stronger than anything you may say or do.
Your children should honor you, for this is right.
Your righteous works are not in vain, for they are pleasing in His sight.

Let's not forget that a mother was once a little girl,
But now she's a woman who brings a beautiful child into the world.
You should be loved, respected, honored and praised.
So strive to be that woman talked about, a Godly mother throughout your days.

Take It From Her: Cautionary Lessons for the Ladies We Love

Still Here
(Inspired by Marvin Sapp's The Best in Me)

I know you didn't have an easy life, but neither did I.
Emotional, sexual and physical abuse, right before my very eyes,
I've been lied on, and took the blunt of the lie just to stand accused.
Yeah, the cycle went on, and I continued being needlessly abused.

Here I am today a survivor and making a difference in this world
Spreading the love of God around me to every man, woman, boy, and girl.
You have been through some storms in your life, too.
You have a testimony of your own just like I do.

For some of you, family members may have disowned you and would never support you.
You thought you were loved, only to find that your parents actually tried to abort you.
You survived rape, divorce, ridicule, or undeserved strife.
You say, why stab me? I can easily stab myself with the trials of life.

For some of you, you tried to do right and still took beatings around you.
No one ever said I love you, and no familial love was there to surround you.
You've wondered within yourself, what's the point of living?
Even though I'm supposed to love others, I feel I'm drained in giving.

For some of you, you had big dreams and could actually feel them,
But the trifling folks, close to you, sided with the devil to steal them.
They wrote you off, said you'd be nothing, said they wished you weren't alive,
But you're still here; the devil tried to kill you, but it was God's will that you survived.

Look at us now, we're alive, and it's by God's grace.
We didn't make it by ourselves; we all need to fall on our face.
He kept us here for a reason; don't take your life for granted.

Take It From Her: Cautionary Lessons for the Ladies We Love

Some of you have sown good seed; so, be patient with the seed you planted.

For it will spring forth; it will truly blossom and yield,
The purpose of your beautiful life – the reason you're still here.

Some people will walk out of your life, but God is in control.
He wants all of you, even your very soul.
He sees the best in you, and He sees the best in me.
Regardless of where you are right now, lift your hands and declare you're free!

Take It From Her: Cautionary Lessons for the Ladies We Love

The Big Payback

I see you my child as you live from day to day.
I know trying to live and do right contains a price that must be paid.
People around you are trying to steer you in all directions,
Keeping you away from the object of your affection.

As the day progresses, obstacles stand in your way.
There are so many words you would like to say.
You hold your peace, and let the knuckleheads be as they are.
Your mind is looking towards me as your eyes stare at the stars.

Your life is tossed and turned, broken and bruised,
While your enemies are getting over, rejoicing when you're being used.
You've been chewed out and demoted as your enemies are getting promoted.
I will repay, and that's a fact; they need to get ready for the big payback.

Because you love and serve me, you're silenced and considered a threat.
I love you so much, and that you should never forget.
Don't take matters into your hands; and whatever you do, don't react.
Your enemies and anti-Christian groups need to prepare for the big payback!

Rest in my care, because it's gonna be alright.
I know you want to fuss, put on your boxing gloves and fight.
Remember one thing that will always be a fact.
I've got you, and I'm the author of the big payback!

Take It From Her: Cautionary Lessons for the Ladies We Love

This Is Me (A Woman's Declaration)
(Dedicated to Jaime Blue)

Hi! Oh, how am I? You want to know my name?
Wait! Do you think this beauty I possess is my claim to fame?
Don't focus on my exterior, get inside my mind.
Don't walk away! Are you scared of what you might find?

Well, this is me, a highly favored woman of the Most High,
Purposed to live for Him until the day I die.
This is me, a conqueror through Christ who loves me.
Don't hate when I say I place no god, but Jehovah, above me.

This is me, a woman who's living in prosperity,
Spiritually and however else God chooses, I say that with sincerity.
This is me; I'm God's child who's been washed in His blood.
With my Redeemer in my heart, I can withstand any fire and any flood.

Can you handle this? Can you get up on my level?
Because I don't have time for fake people, I don't patty cake with the devil.
When you look at me, my desire is that you see
That this is me; predestined and determined to be what He's ordained me to be!

Take It From Her: Cautionary Lessons for the Ladies We Love

What Did I Gain?

I hope none of you ladies ever go through what I went through.
If you're smart, you'll learn from me and your life will be better, too.
I'm currently a homeless advocate, and I'm thankful for God's grace.
Let me tell you what happened, and the past is something I wish I could erase.

I had it all, a gorgeous husband, a daughter and a son.
They were everything to me, but the job I had was second to none.
My dream was to be a CEO of a major corporation.
I was determined to live the dream, even if it meant a separation.

I guess my words were powerful, because I left my family five years ago.
I was promoted instantly from manager to director, then to CEO.
Getting there caused me to compromise a lot of my standards which I now regret,
And I pray this lecture ladies is something you'll never forget.

In order to get to the top, I had to have relations with the director.
He was such a nice guy, and was truly a protector.
Having relations with some board members was what it took to be CEO.
I made it, and I was living the dream, and that was a year ago.

Some board members felt they could take advantage of me after the relations.
They kept threatening me to get involved, but I gained a revelation.
God was asking me, why are you forsaking me?
You had everything that really mattered, and I immediately fell to my knees.

When I told the members "I will not," they fired me on the spot.
They took everything that I possessed, and I truly had a lot.
I ended up homeless until someone reached their hand to me.
They took me in, and what did I gain? God's grace; and these eyes can truly see.

Room 5: The Bedroom

Take It From Her: Cautionary Lessons for the Ladies We Love

A Sister's Commitment to Purity
(Piece and Purity)
(You'll understand after you read)

Hey Baby, how are you?
You're doing fine? I'm doing fine too.
Are you coming over? I can't wait.
Just do me a favor, and don't come too late.

Hey, you brought a movie and what's that in your hand?
Now why did you bring that? Throw them in the garbage can.
Let's set the rules; there will be no intimacy tonight.
Don't get all wild with me, because this sister will win this fight.

Now, can we watch the movie in peace? Thank you, I'm glad you consent.
I was thinking to myself, where your head done went?
Why is your hand on my chest? Get it off of me!
Just because I'm grounded doesn't mean you can take fruit from this tree.

I've got an idea; let me go into my bedroom for a minute.
Before you start to follow me, let me start what I finished.
I have a surprise for you; so stop right there.
Let me nip this in the bud before temptations in your head start running everywhere.

I'm back; oh wait, why are you running towards the door?
Just because I have a pistol for protection doesn't mean I won't knock you to the floor.
I'm just speaking your language; now do you understand?
My purity before God is important; I wouldn't say this to a *Godly* man!

Don't do it for me, do it for your soul and spirit.
I know this is hard for you, but your ears had to hear it.
Now you can try to come back and kill me in return.
My advice to you is better; believe God, repent and turn.

I'm not giving up my purity before I'm married for you or any other man I see.
My relationship with God means too much to me.
So this is my ultimatum, get your life right and start praying with me.
I'm going to remain a woman of God and maintain my commitment to purity.

Take It From Her: Cautionary Lessons for the Ladies We Love

Blame It on Love

Baby, you were all I need and I thank you for all you've done.
But it's time to leave you, and I thank you for telling me I'm your number one.
You've given me some wonderful years, but this is as far as we can go.
Please don't beg me to stay, because there's something I think you should know.

I'm leaving you for someone else, and he knows how to make me feel good.
He touches me in all the right places, and I wish you would've understood.
Sure, he just broke up with his girlfriend, but he's all I need in a man.
Now we could blame it on love, I know the years feel like a one night stand.

There's a thing called temptation that just feels so right to me.
I refuse to believe what you believe now, and I wish you could see what I see.
Now that I've got him, I feel so free in my heart.
And I know that nothing can tear our relationship apart.

You could blame it on love, but I believe fate brought us together.
Now who's to say that I'll be with this new man forever?
Wait, I just had to file a restraining order on this man who I thought did me right.
Well, he showed his true colors after downing a six-pack, and I'm wearing his boxing fight.

Take It From Her: Cautionary Lessons for the Ladies We Love

I Need a Man (Parts 1 & 2)
Explanation written by Brigitte Marshall

(Part 1)
I always feel like I'm in a class by myself.
All my girlfriends have gorgeous men and left the dogs on the shelf.
I don't want a dog; I need a man that will satisfy my cravings.
Don't talk to me about virginity, because that's not worth saving.

I can't stand to go another day without a man.
I don't care if I have to strip for it; I'm going to do whatever I can.
If I have to get plastered to prove I can keep up with the boys,
I'll do that, because my body is screaming, and I don't want to stop the noise.

I know, deep down inside, I'm tired of one night stands,
But you know I'll do anything just to have the comfort of a man.
Yeah, it's selfish, and whorish, but you know, I don't care at all.
So, let me get ready to hit the clubs and just go have a ball.

I'm at the clubs, and hunks of men flock to my dancing feet.
It sure feels good, and now I don't feel like a deadbeat.
All these men order me drinks, and now I'm plastered.
I can't even think straight, and now my heart's beating faster and faster.

(Part 2)
Seven years later, I actually remember the multiple partners that night.
I remember that one night stand with them, and they were out of sight.
But I realize I have to get my life right, not just for my son, but for me.
God, please forgive me, I thought living for lust was the way it was supposed to be.

I have a precious son, and he's adamant when he says to me, "Who is my father?"
I had the men tested to the furious protests, "Why bother?"
"You slept with so many men; anyone could be the father of your son."
Irrespective of who the father is, what's done is done.

Take It From Her: Cautionary Lessons for the Ladies We Love

My son, I wish that you'd prosper as your soul prospers each day. I have something to say to you, and I pray that you learn from the errors of my ways.

Son, you know we go to church to worship God; we go to church to fellowship with others who worship God; I take you to church to hear the preaching/teaching of God's word; so that we can worship Him through song and praise. I want you to know about God in hopes that one day, you will develop a very personal relationship with Him in a way that you will allow Him to lead you; you will ask Him for help in the decisions you make; you will pray and read His word and try to live by what's in His word; you will try to live a life that is pleasing to him so that you can be with Him in heaven one day - and that's what all Christians want. Going to heaven is the goal of all of us who believe in and live for God.

You know that God loved us so much that He sent His Son, Jesus, to die for our sins. And, when Jesus died, and came back to life, all of us became part of God's family; God is our Father, and we are all sisters and brothers in Him. God adopts us into His family when we accept Jesus as our Savior. In saying this, and in knowing that Jesus came so that we could be forgiven, all of us have done some things we shouldn't have done, things that we are ashamed of, things that we don't want anyone to know about because they were stupid mistakes. Because of Jesus, we can be forgiven for our wrongs when we admit to God that we messed up and we ask Him to forgive us, and we repent from what we did. When I was younger, I did some things that I should not have done. God tells us that we shouldn't have sexual relations until we get married; but, I didn't listen to God. I had a lot of boyfriends, and I became pregnant with you, not even knowing which boyfriend was your Dad. I am so sorry for the way I used to act, but God has turned me around. He has blessed me with a fantastic son who I love very much. He has forgiven me for the "wild" lifestyle I was living, and He has changed my heart; so that now I live for Him. I may not really know who your earthly father is, but I do know that you have a Father in heaven who loves you more than you could ever know and who takes care of you every day. You may not be able to see Him with your eyes, but you can feel Him in your heart. He is with you when you go to bed at night; He is with you while you are sleeping; He is with you when you wake up in the morning - and all during the day, He is watching over you. Now, I don't know about you, but I am glad that God is your father, because when you have God on your side, you'll always be "ok". I know this for myself, because God is my father, too; He is a father to everyone who loves Him.

        My son hugs me and declares his love to me.
I try hard not to cry, but I let the tears fall for him to see.
                I thought I needed a man,
        But the MAN I needed now lives within me.

Take It From Her: Cautionary Lessons for the Ladies We Love

Someone to Love
Explanation written by Cynthia Portalatin

My girls and I wanted to go out for a girls' night out.
We decided to check out the club scene and see what it's all about.
While chilling, I noticed one guy and we hit it off well.
To see that we're digging each other is not hard to tell.

After a few days of chatting via telephone, we decide to hook up tonight.
It sure feels good to have someone to love, because my flesh is ready to unite.
He enters my crib, and we're feeling on each other.
We're so fixed on each other that I don't want to be with another

He tells me that he loves me, and he cares for no one else but me.
I fall so deep into his words, and it feels like I'm living in a fantasy.
Our clothes come off, and we're going all the way.
There's no stopping us now; he's mine until the break of day.

Here it is, the next morning, he says, "we can only be friends.
I'm sorry if I've hurt you, but this relationship has to end."
I say, "Was I just a one night stand?" He says, "Yes, but think about this:
You just wanted someone to love you, and I wouldn't doubt this."
I say, "That's beside the point; you don't treat a woman this way,
On some level, I was using you, but you're still going to have hell to pay!"
As he leaves, I start crying and wishing he would die.
I feel so used, and he didn't even tell me good-bye.

God, why did You allow this to happen to me?
If You loved me, You would've shielded me from this tragedy.
I want You to explain to me Your rationale for this.
I'm so angry with You, and saying I hate You is hard to resist.

God silently said to me, "Dear Child, free will is a great gift,
But just like the farmer you must learn to sift;
As not every grain of wheat is fit for your plate,
This lesson if learned will clarify your fate.
Let not this hurt blind you, consume you, nor misguide you.
Instead, embrace the love of my Son, and let it make you new.

Take It From Her: Cautionary Lessons for the Ladies We Love

The devil comes to kill and destroy,
And often comes disguised as a decoy,
Such as a new man whispering sweet nothings in your ear,
Who will tell you lies that only feed into your worst fear!
The emptiness you feel deep within
Can never be satisfied living in sin.
Find refuge in my Word, and put on the armor
That's meant to heal you and make you stronger.
Come know Me, and you will experience great love,
Comparable to none; it comes from heaven above.
I have never left you; I have been here all along,
Waiting patiently for you to hear my joyful song!
I will bring you peace; I will heal your wound.
Trust in Me to love and make your heart anew."

Take It From Her: Cautionary Lessons for the Ladies We Love

The Life of Alyssa Cooper (Parts 1 & 2)

(Part 1)
I met Alyssa Cooper at a bookstore one day.
She was so attractive, and I was glad she passed my way
I made an attempt to speak to her as she smiled at me.
She would grab a latte to drink and a scone to eat.

Alyssa was twenty-thee, and I was twenty-four, and she was ready for love.
I was looking for that too, but wanted to know what she was speaking of.
So we made plans to meet at my crib tomorrow night.
I'm trying to figure out how to make this night special and right.

It's Friday, and I'm making my apartment presentable for her
She knocks at the door, and I'm singing a melody like a bird
Alyssa didn't say hello but proceeds to kiss and hold me.
For what I'm about to say, I hope that she doesn't scold me.

I made a small noise signaling her to stop for a minute.
Hopefully Alyssa will listen to me and above all, let me finish.
I said, "We don't have to do this, considering this is our first time.
I want to respect your virginity, and I ask that you also respect mine."

She said, "Wait, I want to give it up to you, and you're refusing? You must be a punk!"
I think, "I knew this was too good to be true! Now I have to hear this junk!"
She storms out of my apartment, and I say to myself, "What went wrong?"
I thought she would care about our virginity, but now she's gone.

(Part 2)
A month passes by, and I was told she's still searching for someone to give it to.
This is about to change when one of her girlfriends call her out of the blue.
She says to Alyssa, "Girl, I know a man named Stu who's perfect for you."
What Alyssa didn't know was her girlfriend had sex with Stu.

Take It From Her: Cautionary Lessons for the Ladies We Love

She failed to mention that she contracted a disease from Stu as well.
He has herpes and warts on his genitals. Talk about a nightmare from hell.
She goes on to say to Alyssa, "Go on this talk show. The topic is Be My First.
I believe with you going on, and meeting Stu will quench your thirst."

She goes on the show and meets Stu, and they can't wait until after the show.
They check into a local hotel, and he turns the lights in the room down low.
I need to mention that her girlfriends failed to tell her they all had sex with Stu.
They all have the same disease, and they want her to experience this pain too.

As they both climb into the bed, Stu pins Alyssa down as if she was being robbed.
Alyssa's screaming as if she was being chased by the Mob.
Within five minutes there's a pool of blood on the sheets; it looks like a crime scene.
She's relentlessly screaming stop, but he's penetrating like he's living the dream.

After the five minutes of terror, he leaves the hotel as she cries by herself.
She prays to God, "Why was I being selfish, not caring about you or anyone else?
I wish I could have maintained my virginity, for it is a precious thing from you.
Now I need to go get checked to see if I have herpes simplex Type II."

This story is sadly commonplace in the fabric of our society.
So many treat their virginity like it's simple biology.
The life of Alyssa Cooper will never be given back.
She gave up her treasure and got a disease as her reward for one night in the sack!

Take It From Her: Cautionary Lessons for the Ladies We Love

Room 6: The Bridal Suite

Take It From Her: Cautionary Lessons for the Ladies We Love

Don't Waste My Time

I see some women living to be drama queens, striving to be a Baby's mama.
I have no time for the foolishness, no time for unnecessary drama.
I need a man to stand and commit to a relationship.
I believe I'm not asking too much, and that's on a serious tip.

At least one man approaches me week after week.
I check out how they're dressed, and I close in on the words they speak.
The infamous words are spoken to me, "You're so attractive, precious as a pearl.
If you'd share your love with me, I promise you the world."

One man said those lines, and we start dating.
I asked him, "How do you feel about commitment?" He doesn't say anything.
I then say, "Answer the question and why are you hesitating?
I refuse to let you break my heart; I'm not your spring fling!"
After a few minutes, he says, "I guess we won't be intimate, right?"
Of course, I said no, and he leaves my presence like the speed of light.

It seems like men are just pure talk with no action.
Men, don't waste my time if you're just focused on physical attraction.
I'm on a mission, and I'll find a man who's real.
He won't waste my time, and will commit to the marriage seal.

Take It From Her: Cautionary Lessons for the Ladies We Love

He's The One/She's The One

(He's The One)
Let me tell you about this wonderful man in my world.
He loves me so much that he has me fairy-tale dreaming like a little girl.
He's always putting my needs before him; I will always be his baby.
Every time I see him at night, he's praying for my health and my safety.

Whenever he travels, he wants me to go with him to keep me involved in his life.
He trusts me and values me; he makes it easy to be a loving wife.
He pushes me to be my best and supports my talents and calling.
To see him praise the Lord with his might; it's deeper in his love I'm falling.

He believes that behind every successful man is his woman, and I'm his wings.
Oh, God has truly blessed me, and now I have a reason to sing.
I will never leave him, for it would be silly to give him up.
I will honor our marriage vows, and keep love overflowing in his coffee cup.

He's the one who loves me and adores me like a precious flower.
I can't see being without him, not even for one hour.
He's the one whom I will always love and adore forever.
We have so much to impart to each other and the world; we will always be together.

(She's The One)
Let me tell you about this wonderful woman in my life.
She loves me so much that she has consented to be my wife.
She's always putting my needs before her; she will always be my baby.
Every time I see her at night, she's praying for my health and my safety.

Whenever we wake up, I always kiss her face and take her by hand.
She trusts me and values me; she makes it easy to be her husband.
She pushes me to be my best and supports my talents and calling.

Take It From Her: Cautionary Lessons for the Ladies We Love

To see her praise the Lord with her might; it's deeper in her love I'm falling.

I believe that behind every successful man is her woman, and she's my wings.
Oh, God has truly blessed me and now I have a reason to sing.
I will never leave her, for it would be silly to give her up.
I will honor our marriage vows, and keep love overflowing in her tea cup.

She's the one who loves me and adores me like a precious flower.
I can't see being without her, not even for one hour.
She's the one whom I will always love and adore forever
We have so much to impart to each other and the world; we will always be together.

Take It From Her: Cautionary Lessons for the Ladies We Love

Saying Goodbye (The Separation) (Parts 1 & 2)

(Part 1)
Can I talk to you before you turn and walk away?
I know this will be hard, for I'll never see you after today.
I can't repair the mistakes I made,
And I feel like a servant with a debt that can't be paid.

If I could wipe your tears of the wrongs I've done, I would.
I would say I'm sorry, and I love you, only if I could.
If I said I promise to work on my emotions, what does it mean?
The damage is done, and the aftermath of the damage remains to be seen.

Misery is what I will feel as I watch you leave me.
I deserve it; I understand; I have to set you free.
I tried and failed to be a good friend,
And I understand you clearly that our friendship should end.

I know I'm not perfect, and that's on the serious tip,
But I understand that God's kingdom is centered on relationships.
I know I have shortcomings; I have my set of faults.
I may do or say things that bring my life to a screeching halt.

Don't feel sorry for me, and please don't cry.
I can't continue to hurt you; so, we must say good-bye.
One day I will learn to control my emotions,
Without scaring you with my internal explosions.

The more I think about it, there's nothing left to say,
Except I love you, and if we're to survive, I must go away.

(Part 2)
Sure you can talk to me before I walk away,
But know that the blame is not all you: I had my part to play.
I let your sweet whisperings caress me as you backhanded my emotions.
I allowed your gifts to pacify my tears that swelled up like oceans.

So, no, I won't feel sorry for you, but I feel sorry for myself.
I should've said good-bye sooner; for that I blame myself and no one else.

Take It From Her: Cautionary Lessons for the Ladies We Love

I've taken all I can take from you; good-bye is all that can be said.
I wish you could've treated me like you were supposed to, but you lost your head.

Your emotions are so out of control; you deserve to be alone.
Don't write me any e-mails, and don't try to reach me by phone.
Yes, I've made my mistakes, but there's no excuse for you how you treated me.
I'm sorry it has to end this way, but this is how it's going to be.

You're right in that you're not perfect, and you never will be.
How dare you infringe your beliefs on me!
Your faults are inexcusable, and believe me, you're going to pay.
This is the last time you'll see me again, know I love you too, but I must go away!

Take It From Her: Cautionary Lessons for the Ladies We Love

She's Gone (Parts 1 & 2)

(Part 1)
She was everything to me, more than words could ever explain,
But now she's gone from me, and my heart is in so much pain.
We argued over something so petty, that I can't even believe it.
I took the blunt of it, and my ears and heart had to receive it,
Sure, I can take phone calls and texts through the day and even at midnight,
But if I do it in return, I'm inconsiderate and she wants to fight.
I'm exaggerating a little, but I'm rude and in the doghouse.
Once again, we're going through the game of cat and mouse.

I say I'm sorry, and then I'm feeling sorry for what I've done,
But some may say I'm at fault, and some may say you shouldn't have to run.
This really is petty, but either way, she's gone, and I can't help but cry.
I'm a simple man trying to do right, and I repeat, I really do try.
I feel that I should keep my distance, because as usual, I'm to blame.
Whether I apologize or not the outcome is still the same.
She's upset and gone, and there's one thing I need to mention:
I'm scared for the both us; I need to make a date with suicide prevention.

(Part 2)
A few days pass, and I pray for our relationship.
My life is not the same without my backbone, and that's on the serious tip.
I seek counseling, just to talk about how I feel.
The counselor's glad that I'm not at risk, and that my love for her is real.
So, I carry on, worried about her emotional state.
I try calling her in the hopes we can have a clean slate.
My calls keep going to her voicemail, and I get a knock at my door.
The knocks become pounds, and my heart's drumming like never before.

Some of her friends come over and sit me down for what they had to say.
I knew this wasn't going to be pretty, but I wasn't prepared for this rainy day.
They told me she took a bottle of pills, and passed away yesterday.
She wrote a note, and this is what it had to say:
"I love you so much, but I can't stomach this pain much longer.
You made me feel weak, when I was supposed to be stronger.
You are responsible for my suicide and I simply say, 'so long.'"
I'm arrested and may be charged, but either way, she's gone.

Take It From Her: Cautionary Lessons for the Ladies We Love

Skin Deep

Thugged out,
Punked out,
Skinny jeans
Gold teeth –
Can you spot a good brother?

Suit and tie
GQ fly,
Close shave,
Tight fade –
Can you spot a good brother?

Scarred hands,
Dirty nails,
Sweat-stained tee,
Darkened by the heat –
Can you spot a good brother?

Can you spot a good brother or is your vision only skin deep?

The challenge is, ladies; can you spot a good brother?
A brother who's into you and will love you like no other,
Whether thugged out, punked out, wearing skinny jeans,
Whether close shaved, no shave, dirty or dressed clean?
Does he have dirty nails because he worked his fingers to the bone?
Is he living payday to payday; does he have a comfortable home?
Is he an ex-con, decked out with gold teeth and have children everywhere?
Or does he praise God, study God's Word, and treat women with utmost care?

Is he a keeper, or is he only fit for the trash heap?
Tell me ladies, can you spot a good brother, or is your vision only skin deep?

Is your definition of good only a brother from the hood?
Does he only make you swoon if he's born with a silver spoon?
It's so tempting just to fall in love with surface vanity,
But the greatest love is found when you look beyond skin deep.

Take It From Her: Cautionary Lessons for the Ladies We Love

This Feeling

I don't know if you've ever felt this way before,
But this feeling appears periodically at my front door.
It's when you lose your best friend to someone they love,
And on the flipside, you want them to be together like two turtledoves.

Sometimes it makes me crazy; other times I want to be alone.
Just drive long distance and be as far away as I can from home.
Don't get me wrong, I care so much for your happiness,
I'd give up my happiness for you, and endure the unnecessary stress.

This feeling causes within me a warring personality,
Making me feel so far away from reality,
There have been times I wanted to object at a ceremony,
But I hold my peace and deal with the lonely part of me.

I know being friends is as far as we can go,
And "I love you for who you are" is all you need to know.
Just to have that feeling satisfies every bone within me,
And to see your smile is something the world needs to see.

Before you throw comments like, "your time will come" or "it's not your season,"
Think about what you're saying, for there could be a definitive reason.
You probably never had this feeling nor have a reason to care.
That doesn't mean you should pick and choose which burdens you'll bear.

I wish this feeling wouldn't make me so sad,
But every time I look at your beautiful brown eyes, I think of the good times we had.
I pray that God would shower His blessings upon you wherever you go,
And please don't cry as I start to cry, just know that I'll always love you so.

Take It From Her: Cautionary Lessons for the Ladies We Love

When it's Your Turn (This Feeling pt. 2)

When it's your turn, you'll understand
Why I wanted to sit close and hold hands.
When it's your turn, you'll understand
Why I just hummed in the car and kept silent in the van.

When it's your turn, you'll understand
Why I wrote those love notes and slid them under the door.
When it's your turn, you'll understand
Why I struggled to hold on and be pure.

When it's your turn, you'll understand
Every heartache and pain that brought me here.
When it's your turn, you'll understand
Every tear I cried to cover my fears.

So don't begrudge me this day, this moment, this vow, this kiss, this love for two.
For when it's your turn, I'll dance at your wedding too.

Take It From Her: Cautionary Lessons for the Ladies We Love

Wedding Dreams

Lisa and LaShanda are friends and haven't seen each other in three years.
When they reunite at a bookstore, they can't contain their tears.
"Hey LaShanda, you're looking great." "Lisa, you do too."
"Tell me LaShanda, what's been going on with you?"

"Well Lisa, when I last saw you, you didn't have a man in your life
Is that still true? And when will you become some man's wife?
You're much too pretty to be single, are you still maintaining your purity?
I know you're looking for stability and definitely security."

"LaShanda, yes, it's true, and I have maintained my purity.
And yes, my man has to provide me stability and security.
Is that same man still in your life, and are you ready to settle down?
Have you found a church home, or are you chasing men around this town?"

"Lisa, I'm not sure if God will forgive me or if a man can handle me.
I've been involved with so many men, that a good man is hard to for me to see.
I want to do right, and I want to be more like you.
Tell me Lisa, what's your secret and what do I have to do?"

Well LaShanda, I made a vow to God to save myself before jumping in bed.
A man has to respect my decision that there's no nookie before we wed.
In respect to your situation, you can be locked up spiritually until you walk the aisle.
God can forgive anything, trust me, He'll make your life worth while."

Well, I know one day we'll be married to wonderful men and it will feel like paradise,
But we need to live for God daily and who knows? He might give us a surprise:
Men we've prayed for, provided that it's His perfect will for our lives,
But if we stay in His care, we'll definitely be Godly wives.

Take It From Her: Cautionary Lessons for the Ladies We Love

Who Do You Love?

I see you as you enter the bookstore with the same man.
There's a little bit of jealousy, and I camouflage it the best I can
You don't know how much I love you, but maybe you do.
Sometimes I wonder who do you love, but I have a real love for you.

You say you love Me,
But you spend more time with him than with Me,
And you wonder why I'm jealous?
It should be plain to see.

Sometimes you don't notice Me, but you leave your imprint wherever you go.
I'll keep saying it till you understand; I want you to love Me because I love you so.
I don't want to sound conceited when I say that I love you better than anyone,
But that's a fact you can hold me to, it shines brighter than the sun.

I can probably read your mind; you're wondering how much I really love you.
You don't want to commit to Me because you have your pride to hold on to.
Believe Me when I say I can mend your broken heart when it's torn in two.
If you would trust Me with your heart, there's nothing I won't do for you.

My love isn't going anywhere
I've got your name on My hand.
And if you're willing to put My name in your heart,
Forever I'll be your husband.

I know you have so many things to do, but remember I'm here for you.
Whether it's to laugh, cry, or for Me to hold you like no one else could do,
You're the object of My affection, and I want us to be together like a hand in glove
Just know that you have a pending question that needs an answer, "who do you love?"

Take It From Her: Cautionary Lessons for the Ladies We Love

Room 7:
The Secret Place

Take It From Her: Cautionary Lessons for the Ladies We Love

Accept Me Broken (Let Love Make Me Whole)

I have made some mistakes, and I ask that you don't judge me.
Listen to what I say, and please don't act so pretentiously.
I did things in my life that caused me to be talked about and left cold.
Accept me broken, and let His love make me whole.

I'm not proud of what I did; I wish I could take those things back.
I'm just thankful to God that I didn't end up smoking crack.
I thought possessions would make me happy, such as money and gold.
Please accept me broken, and let His love make me whole.

I've been through enough embarrassment, and I can't take anymore.
I ask for your love and support, this is all I ask for.
I let God have all of me, and now I'm being birthed through His love.
Please accept me broken, and let His spirit shine on me from above.

I have been cleansed and washed in His blood, and I see your tears.
Wow, you're crying, God must be breaking your heart and fears.
Now I know your love is real, and I give you my hand to hold.
Thank you for accepting me broken, and allowing His love to make me whole.

Take It From Her: Cautionary Lessons for the Ladies We Love

Grief

Looks like a woman being carried out of service, screaming and crying
Smells like the scent of death hovering above your loved one
Feels like your soul torn asunder in pain
Tastes like food seasoned with Styrofoam
Sounds like a phone ringing at 5am.

Over and over you hear that you'll be okay
But there's not a day of loss that ever goes away
Something triggers your mind again and again
And you find yourself wishing time never had an end
The hope you cling to
The hope that keeps you sane
Is the promise, that in the life to come, you will see them again.

Take It From Her: Cautionary Lessons for the Ladies We Love

I Can't Take This Anymore

When you see me, please don't speak; don't get too close to my life.
I ask that you leave me alone; I don't want any more pain and strife.
I don't know if you understand, or let me be blunt; you probably don't care.
I'll tell those who have an interest; I'm alone and have nothing to share.

I can't take being alone anymore; I want someone to call my own.
I feel like I'm hearing the past, and I agree that I'm so tired of being alone.
I see people in love, and I've been in love before.
But within a year or two, I'm back to loneliness; I can't take this anymore.

Love gives me temporary joy only to be stolen by extreme pain.
Once again I hear the past, and I just want to go out in the rain.
No one can see me cry, and no one can feel sorry for me.
I wish love would let me go, and set my spirit free.

I can't take this anymore; I'm losing whatever's left of my mind.
I really do want to end this cycle, but depression and sadness has me in a bind.
It's funny, because I know the truth, and that love isn't the answer to my situation.
I need to stop living for love, and live to enjoy God's creation.

I know living is hard, and I'm not going to lie about it.
I know love is what I need to understand fully, and I won't doubt it.
Somebody pray for me and for others; we need true love's outpouring on us like never before.
To see us going the way we are today; I won't take this anymore.

Take It From Her: Cautionary Lessons for the Ladies We Love

I Feel So....

Pam is a young adult; she turns men's heads when she walks,
And she loves to hear the chatter as the men gossip and talk.
She decided to flirt and tease them as she passed by,
But one of the guys follows her, and she falls prey to his predatory eyes.

She's mesmerized and gives this guy her number.
He goes back to his friends to gossip, but inside his mind, he wonders,
"Is this a fake number, and will I be able to hit it?
I can be like my boys, add a notch to my belt and quit it."

He calls her, and she gives him directions to where she stays.
He stops by the store to pick up some flowers, and he's on his way.
The first thing he wants to do is sit with her on the couch.
As he's looking into her eyes, his body is starting to slouch.

He moves to kiss her; she kisses him on his ear.
She says, "We can't do this, it's getting hot in here.
Trust me; you need to leave, before I do something I regret."
He says, "Yeah, you're just a tease anyway; someone I'd like to forget."

After he leaves, she says, "I feel so cheap.
I feel so dirty and sinful. I guess what I sow is what I reap.
Lord, please forgive me; I thought this is was real *love*.
I was blind, but now I see that You are love and it comes from *above*."

Take It From Her: Cautionary Lessons for the Ladies We Love

Listen to Me
(Dedicated to at-risk girls at a gender-specific program)

I know you can't see me, but I need your attention.
You can't hear me, and there's something else I need to mention.
I'm the life growing inside of you; therefore, listen to me.
If you don't care about me, then live as if you are carefree.

Listen to me, I have a heartbeat.
Listen to me, I have hands and feet.
Listen to me; I am heaven's gift to you and the world.
Listen to me, because I am your baby girl.

Why do you live your life so carelessly?
Fighting over trivial matters that might possibly injure me.
Why do you harm your body in such a way
To cause you pain; yet, I'm the one who pays?

Listen to me; I am loved, and so are you.
Listen to me; do you love me like you *say* you do?
Listen to me; I am heaven's gift to you and the world.
Listen to me, because I am your baby girl.

I want you to protect me, because you have a responsibility.
Don't *act* like you don't hear me –
saying you don't have the capability.
I need you to be a woman; be who you're supposed to be.
I want you to do it for you, and I ask that you do it for me.

So listen to me, because I look forward to seeing you when I'm due.
Listen to me; I need you to care for me,
because I want to look up to you.
Listen to me; I am heaven's gift to you and the world.
Listen to me, because I am your baby girl.

Small group idea:
Have one person read aloud while everyone else closes their eyes to listen.

Take It From Her: Cautionary Lessons for the Ladies We Love

The Conversion

Ooh, look at him; he's so *fine!*
I need to figure out how to *make* him mine.
I have my agenda, and he's going to convert to *my* beliefs.
I'm going to get him, and my body will be sighing with relief.

I already have a religion, denomination and standards for my man,
And he's going to give me what I want in the best way he can.
I know this might require deception, but men are gullible things.
I speak this man into my life, and seeing him makes my heart sing.

I don't care if he's saved or not, because he's going to worship my ways.
I'm going to convert his thoughts, manner and every word he happens to say.
My friends will be his friends, and that's all he needs in his life.
He should be thankful that *I'm* going to be his wife.

Now that I have him, he's pointing out every mistake *I* make!
It wasn't what I planned, and I need to deprogram him for his sake!
But he won't *budge,* and he's *determined* not to change.
He thinks I'm out of my mind, and my ways are silly and strange.

I gave him an ultimatum: to meet *my* demands or he can be free.
He chose the latter and I said, "You're just a *man* anyway, and you're beneath me.
I can always find another sucker to fall for my deception.
I know you'll be back; and Lucifer told me not to accept your rejection."

Take It From Her: Cautionary Lessons for the Ladies We Love

The Sanctity of Life

Tressa and Tina were sitting on a picnic bench talking about life.
They agreed that life is so full of pain and strife.
Tressa said, "Hey, Tina, you're looking great during your pregnancy."
Tina said, "It's challenging at times, but I love that a life is growing inside me."

Tressa asked, "Have there been times you've thought about abortion?"
Tina said, "Never, that's just as bad as the sin of extortion."
Tressa said, "You know that I've gone through an abortion once before."
Tina said, "I know, and I stood by your side, you're my friend forevermore."

Tressa said, "Thanks, a lot of people gave up on me; I'm glad you're not that way.
I guess they weren't my friends, they always had something negative to say."
Tina said, "Well, a good friend will pray with you, but encourage you through thick and thin.
Sure, there are consequences, and we will live with the consequences of our sin."
Tressa said, "Some people think I'm a sinner and that God will never forgive me.
Sometimes I think they're right, and that I'll live with my scars till eternity."
Tina said, "God is a merciful God, and if you repent with a sincere heart,
He'll forgive you, and will give you a brand new start.
You'll see the child in heaven, if you stay on the straight and narrow way.
Let's continue to encourage each other as we look towards that blessed day."

Room 8: The Delivery Room

Dream Again

When I was little girl, I had such a thirst for the Truth.
Now that I'm older, I reflect back to my youth.
I was full of ideas, full of love and dreams.
What has become of me? I'm just flowing through life like a stagnant stream.

Nothing could stop me from dreaming when I was young.
I was living my life, having so much fun.
The flames of trials came to snuff me out, and now my dreams have died.
What has become of me? It feels like I'm living a lie.

Dear Lord, what would you have me to do? I repent for wasting years.
I know that You are the Lord of the Harvest; so, I give to you my tears.
Open my mind to what is possible; open it to what You want me to do.
I yield my heart, my will and everything I have to You.

Now that You've opened my eyes, I'm giving birth to a dream again.
And since I'm a co-laborer with you, I can say Lord, "Now we may begin!"
What has become of me now? I'm back in sync with the God of all flesh.
Nothing is too hard for Him, and I'm destined for God's best.

Take It From Her: Cautionary Lessons for the Ladies We Love

New Identity

I remember years ago, listening to songs giving women hope.
Songs like "New Attitude," gave me the strength to cope.
I was so proud of those years, but life took a toll on me.
I battled depression and longed for those days of being free.

One day, I grabbed hold of a promise from God's Word.
I wanted to kick myself, because it's a saying I'd always heard.
"If you abide in Me, and My Words abide in you,"
Since I know You are love, I will do what You tell me to do.

I thought I knew what love was, having a man to hold and kiss at night.
I can truly admit that I was wrong, because these men left, far from sight.
Finding refuge in Your Word, and knowing what Your love is to me
Is so refreshing, and it's taking me beyond my definition of "being free."

Lord, I want to meditate on Your Word daily, and do your will.
I will move when you say so; just wait, or stand still.
Look out world, because I'm not the same girl as I used to be.
Coming out of me is an agape love and He's given me a new identity.

Take It From Her: Cautionary Lessons for the Ladies We Love

Pregnant Is My Name

I am pregnant with this dream, and you better believe it's real.
I don't care what people think, and I sure don't care about how they feel.
There will be no miscarriage, and I will carry this baby full-term.
It's not going to grow old and nappy like a faded perm.

This baby I'm carrying is destined for prosperity.
And I'm going to nurture it with faith, hope and charity.
It kicks me periodically and I know it wants to come out now.
There are times I want it delivered now, but I will be patient somehow.

I will wait upon the Lord so I can reap in due season.
I know His promises of patience, which to me is a justifiable reason.
In the meantime, I will do my part in this pregnancy
And have faith in the substance of things hoped for, the evidence of things I can't see.

During this time of patience, I need to keep the weeds out of my lawn.
I will bathe my pregnant child with prayer and supplication from dusk to dawn.
I know the weeds want my child, but I'm not giving it up without a fight.
I'm determined to nurture my child by walking in faith and not sight.

I will hold on and be patient just a little while longer.
I know this is a short-term discomfort, so I will trust His Word to make me stronger.
I believe that as I am patient, I'll soar on eagle's wings.
I will walk and not grow tired; and always have a song of praise to sing!

Where I am at right now is not where I'll be tomorrow.
So I will be patient on His promises, and remove this feeling of sorrow.
I will trust God to do His part will I remain patient on this gift inside of me.
It will be healthy and prosperous and will take me beyond what I can see.

Patience is my name, and I trust God to cover me through this pregnancy.
Because once I give birth, the pain will not compare to the victory.
I know this dream is not for me, but for the King of Glory.
And I believe He will multiply this dream for multitudes to sing, "This is my story!"

Take It From Her: Cautionary Lessons for the Ladies We Love

About The Author

Tremayne Moore, founder of Maynetre Manuscripts, LLC, is an accountant, a writer, a psalmist, a griot, and a spoken word motivational speaker.

He holds a Bachelor of Science Degree in Accounting from Florida Agricultural & Mechanical University and a Bachelor of Science Degree in Management Information Systems from Florida State University.

Tremayne's life can be summarized with a quote from the Apostle Paul from Philippians: Christ shall be magnified in my body; whether by life or by death.

To write Tremayne or to contact him for speaking engagements, address Maynetre Manuscripts, LLC; Post Office Box 14823; Tallahassee, FL 32317; or email him at: tremayne_moore@yahoo.com.

Take It From Her: Cautionary Lessons for the Ladies We Love

www.ingramcontent.com/pod-product-compliance
Lightning Source LLC
Chambersburg PA
CBHW031419040426
42444CB00005B/636